Angel's Dance:
A Collection of Uplifting & Inspirational Poetry

By Lynn C. Johnston

A Whispering Angel Book

Angel's Dance: A Collection of Uplifting & Inspirational Poetry

Copyright © 2006 by Lynn C. Johnston

Revised 2009

All rights reserved under International and Pan-American copyright conventions. No part of this book may be used or reproduced by any means, graphic, electronic, or mechanical including photocopying, recording, taping or by any storage retrieval system without written permission of the publisher except in the case of brief quotations embodied in critical reviews and articles.

ISBN-13: 978-0-9841421-1-8
ISBN-10:   0-9841421-1-8

Whispering Angel Books may be ordered through booksellers or by contacting:

Whispering Angel Books
2416 W. Victory Blvd #234
Burbank, CA 91506
http://www.whisperingangelbooks.com

Printed in the United States of America

Whispering Angel Books is dedicated to publishing uplifting and inspirational works for its readers while donating a portion of its book sales to charities promoting physical, emotional and spiritual healing. If you'd like to learn more about our books or our fundraising programs for your charity, please visit our website: www.whisperingangelbooks.com

DEDICATION

I would like to dedicate this book to all who made it possible. To my grandfather, Cecil, whose love of uplifting and inspirational poetry, was passed down to me. To my mother, Wendy, who actually read each poem and encouraged me to follow this path. To my grandmothers, Dorothy and Grace, who provided support and inspiration. And, lastly, to my son, Sam, who inspired more poems than anyone else and gave me the courage to share my work with others by asking me to read my poems to him instead of a bedtime story.

Contents

A Bravery Pledge 2

A Brickhead Christmas 4

A Child's Imagination 6

A Clear, Bright Star 8

Angel On The Ground 10

Angel's Dance 12

A Popped Balloon 14

A Tally Mark 16

Beautiful 18

Because You Mean So Much To Me 20

Child In The Picture 22

Dancing With Santa 24

Dreamland 26

Evolution 28

Faith 30

Glimmer Of Hope 32

If You Gave Your Heart To Me 34

I Love You 36

Infatuation 38

In Your Arms 40

I've Had It With Reality 42

I Wonder 44

Keeper Of The Flame 46

My Little Superstar 48

My Millennium Wish 50

Obsession 52

Ode To Tennyson 54

O Spirits Gather Closely 56

Romance 58

Sleep Tight, My Little Darling 60

Smiling From Above 62

Something Did Survive 64

The Mistletoe 66

The Night 68

The Night Breeze 70

Three-Dimensional Me 72

To Achieve You Must Believe 74

To See The Night Sky 76

Truly Blessed 78

We'll Never Be Too Far Apart 80

Winter Days 82

You Are My Hero 84

You Make Me Smile 86

You've Become A Part Of Me 88

About The Author 91

A Bravery Pledge

When you think of bravery, what comes to your mind? If you're like most, it probably conjures up images of a firefighter running into a burning building to save a helpless victim... or maybe you envision a soldier in a fierce battle defending his country against a ruthless enemy. While they are certainly brave, I cannot deny the courage displayed by ordinary people facing their deepest and darkest fears head on. For me, my greatest fear is the possibility of letting fear stand between me and my goals – quite a rock and a hard place, huh?

"A Bravery Pledge"

Some think bravery is living without fear
But that is not true
Bravery is living despite the fear
Doing what needs to be done
Even though you're scared to death
Some can stand on the sidelines of life
And be content with what could have been
But never was and that is not me

I will not look back at the end of my life
Thinking of what could have been
I vow to live my dreams no matter what
I will stand up and be counted
Even when I'm one of the few
Or standing all by myself
I will proudly state before God and all who see
This is who I am and what I want to be
I will stand proudly in the batter's box
On the baseball field of my dreams
And I will not cower at the thought of being hit
Or feel ashamed if I should strike out
If I do not achieve all that I desire
It will not be for lack of courage or effort
I will go down swinging
As if my life depended on it
But if all I want is meant to be
Then I will hit a home run
That will not only echo in my heart and mind
But in all of those who were destined
To witness my success
And maybe in that moment
Courage will be found in another
Searching for the strength to be brave

A Brickhead Christmas

Music has always played an important role in my life. In fact, my mother once told me that I could dance even before I walked. One day my love of music form drew into the world of Jim Brickman, aka "America's New Romantic Piano Sensation." His fans, known as "Brickheads," enjoy the romantic piano ballads he performs with the help of his long-time friends, Anne Cochran and Tracy Silverman. After following Jim and company on his Christmas tour for three consecutive shows, I got into the Christmas spirit with a little holiday offering of my own.

"A Brickhead Christmas"

Twas just weeks before Christmas and all through the land
Awaited eager Brickheads with tickets firmly in hand
They came to the venue with great anticipation
Of seeing Jim Brickman, Romantic Piano Sensation

As Jim took to the stage, their eyes started to shine
Then he melted their hearts with his Christmas Valentine
He played "The Gift" and "Peace" but that was only the start
He also sent a little Christmas to those who were apart

His fingers danced on the keys playing his Brickmanized hits
His arm flew back so fast as if in a fit
He smiled and spoke of a time long ago
Spending his winters in Cleveland shoveling snow

Tracy was there with his cool violin
Rockin' the house where every fan wore a grin
Anne Cochran was singing the classics they'd know
That filled up each heart with a warm loving glow

It seemed in no time the show came to an end
And Jim took a bow and waved goodnight with his friends
Merry Christmas they said as they got on their bus
And Happy New Year to you from each one of us

A Child's Imagination

Watching my son play with some neighborhood children at our local park inspired "A Child's Imagination." The children played and leaped from the equipment transforming into one character after another with equal conviction. It reminded me that with a little faith and imagination we have the ability to reinvent ourselves at will.

"A Child's Imagination"

A child's imagination
Is something special to behold
Inanimate objects come to life
Creating new stories to be told

"Ahoy there, matey," he called out to me
From a cardboard box
"I found some buried treasure, Mom"
His hands full of twigs and rocks

He sings his favorite songs to me
Cause he's a rock star in his mind
And as a mighty Power Ranger
He fights those who live a life of crime

A hockey pro and baseball star
Are what he'd like to be
He leaps and yells pretending
He's Tarzan swinging from a tree

He's a soldier and an astronaut
A Pokémon master in his dreams
A gymnast on the monkey bars
Winning a gold medal for his team

His imagination beckons me
To all that life could be
If I keep on dreaming
Despite whatever I may see

A Clear, Bright Star

In the movie, "An American Tail," the character of Fievel dreams of being reunited with his family. He takes great comfort in knowing that even though they aren't physically together, he is still loved and missed. Like him, I find great comfort in knowing the people I care about could be looking up at the night sky and seeing the same star, thinking of me as I'm thinking of them. It reminds me that emotional distance often takes a greater toll on our relationships than physical miles. "A Clear, Bright Star" represents a cosmic meeting place for our spirits, and a reminder out of sight does not have to mean out of mind.

"A Clear, Bright Star"

Looking at the night sky
I search for a clear, bright star
To relay how much I miss you
And how dearly loved you are

I send up to it a kiss goodnight
And a wish for dreams so sweet
A warm embrace that fills your heart
Until it makes you feel complete

I send up my faith in all you do
To keep you strong within
And a cheerful smile
So sadness never can set in

I send up to it my heart and soul
So you'll never feel alone
With a prayer
You will be safe and sound
And that you'll soon be home

I send up my fervent wish
That you'll know my love is true
And when you see a clear, bright star
You'll know what it holds for you

Angel On The Ground

One chilly night, my young son crawled into my bed and we cuddled under the covers. As we talked one of us said to the other, "You're my angel on the ground." I honestly don't remember who said it, but I loved the thought that angels could be guiding us here on Earth as well as from above. Our "angels" don't just comfort us during the rough times; they uplift our spirits and triumph in our victories along with us. The phrase stuck in my head for months before it gave birth to this poem.

"Angel On The Ground"

When the world begins to crumble
And my wings can't take off in flight
Your gentle love envelopes me
Until I know I'll be alright

Somehow you lift me up
And help me learn to fly again
You guide me with a love
That knows no boundaries or an end

And when the world is on my side
Life goes as I think it should
You're the first to say, "Let's celebrate"
Or "I always knew you could"

You're my angel on the ground
My slice of Heaven from above
The special gift God sent me
So I'd always feel His love

You're such a cherished gift to me
I can't tell you what you're worth
Except to say you're living proof
Angels do live here on Earth

Angel's Dance

Angel's Dance was inspired by an incredibly beautiful song written and performed by Jim Brickman. "Circles" immediately entranced me, drawing me into my living room from the kitchen. Its hypnotic melody gave me a new understanding of how mythical sailors could be lured to their deaths by a beautiful siren's song. I replayed "Circles" countless times that day before I felt an overwhelming desire to write a poem. I sat with pen in hand still unsure of what would come out, but the inspiration of that song lured me into the most magical writing experience I've ever had. To this day whenever I hear "Circles" or read "Angel's Dance," I am transported back to that special day.

"Angel's Dance"

Above the moon and beyond the stars
Through the Heavens I did fly
Until a little angel's laugh
Caught me by surprise

She giggled as she flew away
I followed in pursuit
And found her dancing on a cloud
While another played a flute

I spied her joyful dance
As she twirled herself around
Her wings fluttered in the breeze
Lifting her gently off the ground

She beamed inside the glowing rays
Of the setting sun
And she ended with a pirouette
When her dance was done

As her music softly faded
She blew a kiss my way
Then hovered for a moment
Before she slowly flew away

A Popped Balloon

"A Popped Balloon" is a recounting of my four-year-old son's trauma over the loss of his balloon. He collapsed into my arms and wept with a depth of emotion you might expect from the death of a loved one. Initially I was confused by his grief, but I soon became envious over his ability to let out his pain without regret or apology -- an ability we often lose as we grow into adulthood.

"A Popped Balloon"

I looked into his crying eyes
His heart so wracked with pain
Large, wet tears rolled down his face
So tortured and so stained
His aching frame fell to my arms
He wailed out loud and long
No false pride or fake facade
No reason to be strong
What, I thought, could cause this pain
To my child's grieving heart
Surely something horrible
Was tearing him apart
"My balloon went pop," he cried out to me
As the words caught in his throat
So much sadness, so much pain
Over a thing that ceased to float

Then I thought how as adults
We hide our inner pain
All the struggles we go through
Just to play our little games
We can't be weak or feel alone
We can't be scared or lost
We must be strong and proud and brave
No matter what the cost
What joy must be in crying free
Without remorse or shame
No apology need be made
Nor pledge that things will change
Why can't we mourn our popped balloons
That steal away our joy
Why can't we let out daily grief
Just like my little boy

A Tally Mark

"A Tally Mark" is based on my belief that no uplifting moment is ever lost in our subconscious. We record each moment where we find love, happiness, peace, beauty and solace. It then etches a mark in our heart that often outlives the memory of the event. When a wonderful memory is recalled, it becomes a cherished gift that we get to unwrap in our minds over and over again. But even if it becomes lost in our consciousness and we never think of it again, it still has the ability to leave an indelible mark behind.

"A Tally Mark"

Every smile, every laugh
Leaves a tally mark behind
A residue of happiness
Enriching a heart and mind
Every loving gaze
Brings solace to the soul
Leaving peace and quiet
When fear's been in control
Every sympathetic ear
And every caring touch
Lingers in the spirit
To provide a needed crutch
Even a brief moment
Can become a special gift
A memory we can treasure
That will comfort and uplift
But if that moment is forgotten
And never brought to mind
It still touched a life with kindness
Leaving a tally mark behind

Beautiful

When I think of beauty, it usually brings to mind something nature has to offer – a sunset or a rainbow. But without taking anything away from Mother Nature, I realized a loving gaze and genuine smile had the ability to take my breath away faster than anything else ever designed by nature.

"Beautiful"

I simply love to look at you
There's no sight I'd rather see
Nothing in this world compares
You are so beautiful to me

I'd sooner miss a rainbow
Arcing softly through the skies
Than I would the gentle hues
That grace your lovely eyes

I'd sooner miss a shooting star
Or fireworks display
Than the special smile
That always brightens up my day

I'd sooner miss a sunset
Streaking purple, red and gold
Than the beauty of the face
I am so lucky to behold

Because You Mean So Much To Me

Many people look upon missing someone as a negative emotion. I, however, view it as a wonderful reminder of how much someone really means to us. Think about how many people walk in and out of your life relatively unnoticed – co-workers, neighbors, even the teenager bagging the groceries at the market. Do you miss them when they're not around? Well, don't feel bad; we cannot be emotionally invested in everyone we meet. Take the time to appreciate the fact that we only miss the people we care about.

"Because You Mean So Much To Me"

When you left
I didn't know
How much I'd miss you
Or how that void would grow
Each day that passes
Takes a part of my heart
Each tear that falls
Reminds me we're apart
But in my pain
I can find a smile
Because I know
All the while
I would not miss you
If you didn't mean so much
I would not shed a tear
If I didn't need your touch
I can't wait to throw my arms around you
And feel your strong embrace
I can't wait to look into your eyes
And gently kiss your face
Missing you is difficult
But it also makes me see
I need you in my life
Because you mean so much to me

Child In The Picture

As children we all had many dreams and expectations for the future. Life, however, often has a different plan for us leaving its own unexpected joys and heartaches. I've looked at pictures of myself at a young age and others wondering what we would have thought had we known what was to come.

"Child In The Picture"

Child in the picture
Sweetness radiates from thee
Rapture fills your heart
As you imagine what could be

The world will be your oyster
Thrilling notions fill your head
You nestle in their visions
While dreaming silently in bed

Child in the picture
Did the world do right by you
Was the pleasure worth the pain
That nearly tore your heart in two

Were you protected from the evil
That befell so many hearts
Were you sanctioned from above
To overcome and stand apart

Child in the picture
Can you still dream of what might be
Now that you're no longer
The young girl that once was me

Dancing With Santa

When you were young, did you ever fantasize about seeing Santa Claus on Christmas Eve? I made numerous attempts over the years to catch Santa in the act of delivering his bounty of gifts for me and my brothers. I'd stay up late and sneak downstairs once everyone else had fallen asleep. While I did discover the presents he left behind, I never managed to catch him in the act. With those fantasies in mind, I wrote this poem on Christmas Day 2007 with the intention of conjuring up all of the wonderful feelings of that time.

"Dancing with Santa"

It was Christmas Eve night and all were asleep
When I crept down the stairs in hopes of a peek
Of Santa's descent through our brick fireplace
With toys just for me, wrapped up with ribbons and lace
My eyes were aglow with excited delight
When his boots and red suit appeared in my sight
He placed all the presents under the tree
Then turned around quickly and smiled at me
He said, "I've got something for you I know you'll adore"
He gave me a gift and then smiled once more
I tore off the paper, got the ribbon untied
It was a small music box with a ballerina inside
As the music started to play, Santa asked for a dance
Then I stood on his feet and we began to prance
Santa spun me around as I giggled with glee
We danced all through the house, just Santa and Me
We danced around the tree with its twinkling lights
Oh, how I loved dancing with Santa on that Christmas Eve night

The ballerina twirled with us as we danced to her song
But soon Santa grew tired and it wasn't too long
Before the time came when Santa said he must leave
As he started to turn, I grabbed onto his sleeve
I begged him to stay and I started to cry
"Just one more dance then," he said with a sigh
Santa spun me around as I giggled with glee
We danced all through the house, just Santa and Me
We danced around the tree with its twinkling lights
Oh, how I loved dancing with Santa on that Christmas Eve night
Then Santa said firmly, you must now go to bed
Tomorrow is Christmas, there's much fun still ahead
As I went up the stairs I knew I'd always remember
Dancing with Santa that special night in December

Dreamland

Lullabies and childhood stories help me connect to both my child and my own past memories. As a mother, I would like to be the white knight capable of protecting him from any menacing demons he might face -- real and imagined. I know that is impossible, but "Dreamland" suspends that harsh reality for a brief moment.

"Dreamland"

As I watch you sleeping
I pray sweet dreams fill your head
And your heart soars high on angels' wings
As you lie quietly in bed

May you drift off to a land
Full of enchantment and delight
Where every rainbow has a pot of gold
Glistening in the bright sunlight

A place where heroes never stumble
Riding bravely on white steeds
And nothing is impossible
As long as you believe

But should a ghost or demon
Ever disturb your peaceful sleep
Know that I'll be by your side
To slay it at your feet

Then I'll hold you close
And rock you gently in my arms
Until you're safely back in Dreamland
With all its magic and its charms

Evolution

Although it is hard to embrace the unknown, nothing ever stays the same. "Evolution" speaks to the inevitability of change and how we must accept its ever-constant presence in our lives, whether we like it or not.

"Evolution"

Mountains worn by wind and rain
Leave rolling hills of green
Old buildings crumble to the ground
Replaced with towers slick and sheen

From cocoons emerge the butterflies
Rivers cut new paths through land
The ocean laps against the shore
Destroying castles made of sand

The old are lost and mourned for
As new babies take their place
Fall leaves tumble from a branch
Dying gently with such grace

Friends turn into lovers
And old lovers into friends
Evolution's ever present
Changing always without end

Faith

Have you ever met someone who had given up on their dreams? When life has smothered their last gasp of hope? Sometimes they are angry and bitter; sometimes they are just an empty shell of the person they once were. Having faith can be difficult when everything seems to conspire against you, but losing faith often winds up killing a lot more than just a dream.

"Faith"

His fragile bones sat in a chair
With an old photograph in hand
In it he was lean and tall
A suave and handsome man
Back then his hair was full and blond
Instead of thinning gray
He once was strong and virile
And his smile could brighten any day
In his youth he was indestructible
Spirited and carefree
He believed he could do anything
And he knew how his life would be
He remembered his enthusiasm
With his heart so full of faith
There wasn't any room for fear
He was surely in God's good grace
But his best-laid plans were not to be
And the failures took their toll
Doubt riddled through his body
Destroying his spirit and his soul
Soon he gave up trying
And worse, he gave up on himself
His faith had taken its last breath
And he put his dreams upon a shelf
He mourned the man he used to be
As the tears rolled down his face
How different life just might have been
If he had only kept his faith

Glimmer Of Hope

Hurricane Katrina left an indelible mark in the late summer of 2005. The devastation left thousands without homes or jobs, and for some, without loved ones. Despite all of the tragedy, not all of the stories and images on the television news were heartbreaking. In a time of such horrific loss, people from all over the country and the world pulled together in hopes of restoring some of what Mother Nature so violently destroyed. It reminded me of what can happen when a glimmer of hope smolders among the ashes.

"Glimmer Of Hope"

Shattered lives and shattered hearts
Shattered worlds torn apart
Tattered clothes and tattered dreams
Life blown asunder, so it seems

From the dark of night, all is lost
Devastation too high to count the cost
Yet amidst all the misery that abounds
A glimmer of hope can somehow be found

In an open heart and an outstretched hand
A compassionate smile helps us understand
We're not alone in our desperate plight
Someone can help us win our fight

With a little faith and a little hope
We'll find some peace and a way to cope
Thanks in part to someone who cared
Who was willing to give and willing to share

If You Gave Your Heart To Me

Falling in love can be a time of great joy and great insecurity. This poem conveys the assurance of acceptance and protection from heartbreak that can help a fledgling relationship grow and endure.

"If You Gave Your Heart To Me"

If you gave your heart to me
You'd never need to be afraid
That I would mistreat it
Or refuse the love it gave

Your heart would be a cherished gift
I'd watch over every day
And I would never give it cause
To feel dishonored or betrayed

I'd promise that I'd always
Keep it safe and sound and warm
I'd protect it as I would my own
Against life's raging storms

I'd try to heal the painful scars
Left by those who were unkind
I'd replace its fears
With hopes and dreams
And a faith that's never blind

I would feel so very lucky
If you gave your heart to me
Nobody in this world would feel
More grateful than I'd be

I Love You

Although I had not intended to write poetry, the inspiration for this poem could not be expressed any other way. It became my first serious attempt at mastering the art form. The fine line between friendship and love is a tenuous state at best filled with fear and trepidation. These emotions came to the surface in the poem that reintroduced me to writing after a four-year hiatus.

"I Love You"

You've been my loving friend; you've come to mean so much
I've reveled in your smile and your gentle touch
You've brushed away my tears; I've soothed your aching heart
We've danced and laughed and played
A friendship special from the start
But lately something's changed for me and silent I can't be
Why is it words come hard when feelings flow so easily
To put it simply, "I love you," but please don't turn away
Cause there's so much in my heart I really need to say
Before I've said, "I love you" to a heart not so inclined
I've crumbled to that deafening silence that was left behind
A feeling strong and pure yet full of desperate shame
I vowed I'd never hence be filled with such a pain

I don't know if you love me back; only you know if you do
But whatever's in your heart, please know that I'll get through
For even if you turned away and walked right out in strife
I always will be grateful you were the love of my life
As I've grown to love you I've been happy for each day
And I'll always keep this fire inside no matter what you say
This fire's warm and cozy for the days I am alone
A memory rich with love even if it's just my own
My love for you is stronger than my fear you'll turn away
I can only wish and hope that you'll want to stay
Please don't say you love me just to ease my troubled soul
For you have been my beacon as my heart's lost all control
But if somehow I've touched you too deep inside your heart
Let's begin a love affair that can't be torn apart

Infatuation

"Infatuation" was born of a traumatic high school experience. Are there any other kind? Through that experience though, I learned something about people. When we first meet someone, anyone, we immediately form an opinion about them. If we have a positive reaction, we'll see them as attractive, smart, charming and we'll presume they have all the qualities we like. If we have a negative reaction, we'll see them as unattractive, dumb and unpleasant with the qualities we don't admire. With the limited information we have, we fill in the blanks with our own definition of who we think they are. As I learned the hard way, that's all well and fine as long as we can adjust our perceptions along the way and learn accept them for who they really are. When that doesn't occur, a painful disconnection with reality can leave both people disillusioned.

"Infatuation"

As you look into my eyes, there's a smile on your face
You brush against me gently then stand awkwardly in place
I get that funny feeling and the rumors have begun
Your infatuation's blossomed and my instinct is to run
Now it's not that I'm afraid of love; in fact the opposite is true
But infatuation's different and I dread it like the flu
It always comes on strong pretending
That true love's your destiny
You think you've found a perfect mate
And the love that's meant to be
Somehow I'm put upon a pedestal by one
Who thinks I'm just the best
Until he soon discovers I'm not much different from the rest
I don't know when or where I'll fall from his pedestal so high
Once he sees I'm only human; I get mad and yell and cry
The problem's been he can't see me or hear the words I say
He gets so wrapped up in his ideal,
He hears "night" when I say "day"
How can love start or have a chance if he's blind to who I am
He'll never see my weaknesses or know when to hold my hand
I never feel I'm needed to support his fantasy
I might as well go on my way God knows he won't miss me
I'd walk away and leave my cardboard figure in my place
Then I'd return to find he'd married it
And see three kids around my waist
So here's the lesson I have learned
And one I hope you will remember
When someone ignites a spark leaving
That warm and glowing ember
Don't anticipate their answers; really listen to what they say
And when their words surprise you,
Let the chips fall where they may
Know their faults and weaknesses, not to belittle or abuse
But so you'll know to be there when their spirit has been bruised
When you see the person beneath the image that you love
You may find out they're better than the person you dreamed of

In Your Arms

Whether young or old, we all need a place to escape when life gets to be too much. Sometimes the only outlet we have is deep within our imagination – a place where life is always sweet and gentle and there is never a trace of fear or despair. When we are young, it seems so much easier to believe that everything will be fine; as we grow older we are forced to confront the reality of that wish. At least when we are able to find comfort and support in the loving arms of someone special, we may be able to recapture a little bit of our lost naivety.

"In Your Arms"

As a child I used to dream
Of a magical place where no one would scream
Where the sunshine warmed my freckled face
And memories of pain could all be erased

Where the soft breeze would blow through my hair
And I could walk without a care
Where the sand would seep between my toes
And I could hide from my painful woes

As the water lapped against my feet
My heart could recover from hurt and defeat
Swaddled in a blanket, the world shut out tight
No matter the pain I would be all right

A place that only existed in my young mind
That as I grew up became harder to find
The older I got I couldn't pretend
And wounds left by life needed much more to mend

That world disappeared as age took its place
Until the day it returned in your sweet embrace
In your arms I feel safer than I ever did then
And I can thank God I need no longer pretend

I've Had It With Reality

After writing "My Millennium Wish," I wanted to revisit the issue of an altered reality. Mine wasn't really working out. Since I had taken such a serious tone with the other poem, I wanted to make sure I addressed this poem with a lighter, if not funny, approach. For nearly two weeks, I wrote down everything I could think of that would make my life ideal. Years later, it still works for me.

"I've Had It With Reality"

I've had it with reality; it's simply not for me
So instead I'll trade it in for what I'd like to see
Diets are forbidden now 'cause everyone is thin
And broccoli's discovered to be the latest carcinogen

Hot tubs and Jacuzzis replace bathtubs that are small
And all I want is always on sale at my favorite mall
I'm completely irresistible to the men that I desire
And money quickly grows on trees
So I can kick back and retire

PMS does not exist and checkout lines are short
Every nasty muttered slight has just the right retort
Celebrities and heads of state line up to shake my hand
And on the beach my bathing suit never fills with sand

We all now get what we deserve because life is just and fair
And cheesecake's now a health food
There are no more bad days for my hair
It rains only when I want it to and jet planes are all on time
And now I'm never at a loss for the perfect word or rhyme

My kids obey my orders and they always clean their room
Housework simply does itself; I never need to touch a broom
I've had it with reality, I quit as of today
So here is where you'll find me if I can keep the truth away

I Wonder

I wrote "I Wonder" with the belief that there is someone out there for everyone. Whether or not we ever meet or recognize them in our fast-paced world of instant gratification is another issue. Over the years, I have spent time wondering about the man meant for me. Who is he? What is he doing? What will we have in common? Will I be able to get him to stick around long enough to help him realize just how spectacular I really am? What will we gladly endure because we think the other person is worth it? Will he leave his clothes on the bathroom floor or his shoes in the middle of the living room? Does he snore... or drool in his sleep? Is he wondering about me too? And am I the only one asking all these questions?

"I Wonder"

I stand alone and stare upon a night so clear and bright
And wonder if just maybe too you're seeing the same sight
Are you staring at my star and wishing you'll find me
Or are you with someone tonight unaware you'll soon be free

I wonder if you think of me as much as I do you
And if you're close or far away and if your eyes are blue
I know you're out there somewhere although we've yet to meet
Will it be through our good friends or accidentally on the street

I wonder what you look like
And if we'll know right from the start
That we were meant to capture each other's loving heart
Will you like my favorite foods or have the same pet peeves
Will you like cold, rainy nights or to play in fallen leaves

I wonder of your dreams and goals and if they're close to mine
Wouldn't it be wonderful if we could help each other shine
I wonder what you're doing now and hoping it's much fun
Watching an old classic film or maybe playing in the sun

I wonder who's been in your life; who's made you who you are
Did they give you all you need or leave you with a scar
Will you like my favorite songs and want to dance with me
Will you promise not to laugh if I can't sing along in key

I wonder if the day will come
I'll look upwards to the sky
Just to look back down again
To see you standing by my side

Keeper Of The Flame

This poem is dedicated to my grandmother, Dorothy – otherwise known as Mimi. She was my favorite relative as a child and we had a very special relationship. In fact, I was her favorite grandchild – but let's not mention that to my brothers or cousins. It will just be our little secret. I have so many wonderful memories, like when she used to sing to me or when she used to let me crawl into her bed during nap time – and we'd snuggle. Sadly, during the last few years of her life, she suffered from dementia. Debilitating like Alzheimer's disease, it robs the mind of its wisdom and memories. She didn't even know who I was the last time I saw her. I can only hope that she can remember now from the other side.

"The Keeper Of The Flame"

Through the years we've shared so much
The laughter and tears and each loving touch
The moments we had left its mark on my soul
All of life's celebrations and the heartbreaking blows
Were etched in my memory and I thought in yours, too
Until this horrific disease robbed it from you
As your memories grow dim and you don't know my name
I will vow to remember, I'll be the keeper of the flame
Our memories will thrive if I've got anything to say
And I'll relay our cherished stories until my dying day
So all will know just how much we once shared
And that nothing can rob us of the way that we cared
I'll remember for you and often pray for a time
When the flame of our memories can be rekindled in your mind

My Little Superstar

At the tender age of four, my son began having great illusions of super stardom. His fascination with the songs he heard on the radio led him to become a great singer on the stage: the stage of his imagination. I delighted in his performances as I spied on his show through the bedroom door. "My Little Superstar" is a literal recounting of my favorite concert experiences, courtesy of my son.

"My Little Superstar"

He takes the stage and holds the mic
Close up to his lips
He sings of love both lost and found
As he bumps and grinds his hips

But he doesn't have a record deal
Or albums made of gold
He's just my singing superstar
Who's all of five years old

His stage: atop a full size bed
His spot: an old flashlight
He dances in the mirror
As I gleam with such delight

His songs: taped off the radio
And a few he learned from me
He works so hard to learn the words
And tries to sing in key

His costume: that's the topper
As he belts out to his tape
Superman pajamas,
Complete with feet and cape

He is my little superstar
Who knows where this will go
But for a singing five-year-old
He puts on quite a show

My Millennium Wish

Written on December 31, 1999 and January 1, 2000, "My Millennium Wish" was inspired by the worldwide television coverage of the changing of the millennium. With all of the religious and political discord in the world, I found it fascinating that there seemed to be no arguments over the celebration of this event. It seemed no matter what the culture, virtually very nation marked this passage with party favors, champagne, fireworks and kisses. Why then, I asked myself, can't we agree on something as simple as human decency, respect and compassion? This millennium is still young, and hopefully we can make a change for the better.

"My Millennium Wish"

As I look back at the past, I'm amazed at what we've done
We've put men on the moon and the computer age has begun
Automobiles in every garage, TVs in each home
Fax machines and VCR's, compact discs and mobile phones
We've seen the best man has to give through nature's adversity
But we've also seen man's evil side; his cruel inhumanity
With the bomb, we've learned to kill those we've never seen
We've hunted and killed the innocent to fulfill our evil schemes
We've judged those who were different by birth or just by choice
We've freely scorned not knowing them
Or listening to their voice
We no longer know our neighbor
And we've lost track of faithful friends
Guns and knives have replaced our words
Violent means to deadly ends
My millennium wish is to focus on the people in this world
Let's put aside our judgments and embrace each boy and girl
Instead of seeing differences and all that could divide
Let's look for commonality throughout this world so wide
Let's reach out to our neighbors and the sick and elderly
Let's make sure every child's loved, living happy and carefree
Let's make this world a cleaner place
Without pollution or disease
Let's not have to worry about what's in our air and in our seas
Let's value people over money and make sure everyone is fed
Let's see they have a warm, safe place
And a strong roof over their head
Let's try to leave this world a little better than it was
And hope the next millennium
Will have more compassion and more love

Obsession

Obsession was written at a frustrating time in my life when problems, concerns and desires had enveloped my mind. It seems the harder you try to avoid your problems, the easier it is for them to find you. With tongue planted firmly in my cheek, I decided to address the issue head on.

"Obsession"

When thoughts run through my head
It can be a blessing or a curse
A blessing if a problem solved, but often it's much worse
Thoughts or feelings from the blue that sit and stew for days
Often leaving me confused and in a blurry haze
They're uninvited visitors that just won't go away
Always needing company most minutes of the day
Seldom when those feelings come they ever take quick flight
Often mine arrive with a suitcase in the night
They pretend they won't be staying long,
But that simply isn't true
At first light their things arrive brought in by moving crew
Now sometimes it's for the best; they drive me towards my goal
But often they just twist my mind
And suck the spirit from my soul
They rob the oxygen from my brain, so nothing else survives
Leaving all else dying while it lives and breathes and thrives
Sometimes I get to take control and they leave without a trace
But it never seems to be too long before new ones take its place
My comfort is the knowledge, and thank God, it can be said
At least I don't hear voices coming from my head

Ode To Tennyson

The great poet, Lord Tennyson, once wrote it was better to have loved and lost than to have never loved at all. An ardent supporter of his view, I know that warm, loving memories can provide great comfort even after a relationship has ended. It is often the possibility of having those kinds of moments again that helps us take another chance on love.

"Ode To Tennyson"

Some would rather be alone
Than to have loved and lost someone
They say it's just not worth the pain when all is said and done
They fear that if they shared a love
With one who's soon departed
It would leave more pain and heartache than if it never started
But being Love's proponent and someone whose felt it all
Let me tell you why I think it's really worth the fall
Whether you've had love gone wrong
Or been alone for all your years
You know that haunting heartache
That leaves pain and scars and tears
Without a love you're always safe
No one can play with your emotions
But if you give yourself to love, it fills you with devotion
You'll have the chance to share your dreams
And you'll feel you're understood
You'll find an inner strength and warmth that feels so good
You'll whisper things into their ears
And share sweet kisses in the night
You'll snuggle close together convinced this love is right
You'll feel their breath upon your skin and look into their eyes
And share a laugh at funny things that take you by surprise
You'll drink champagne and maybe too
Make love by candlelight
You'll dance to slow, soft music and gaze up at starry nights
You'll have your share of sadness too but now you're not alone
You have a caring shoulder and someone to call your own
For those who never take a chance on love that comes their way
Never have those memories to ease their empty days
Years may pass and you might find that the love
You've always shown
Has not made them turn away; in fact, their love has grown
But if the worse should come to pass
And your love comes to an end
At least you'll have love's memories
Which will help your heart to mend

O Spirits Gather Closely

In time of need we should connect with a power greater than ourselves, whatever we define that power to be. I believe that if we take the time to listen, we will receive the answers we need to help guide, strengthen and empower us to live the lives we were meant to have.

"O Spirits Gather Closely"

O Spirits gather closely
And wrap me in your wings
Let me feel you deep inside
Infuse the love and faith it brings

O Spirits gather closely
Shine your light to lead my way
Soothe my troubled soul
And repair my feet of clay

O Spirits gather closely
Let me know you'll never leave
Guide me with your gentle voice
Give me the courage to succeed

O Spirits gather closely
Help me not to go astray
Or lose the dreams that inspire me
To fight on another day

Romance

So often when people think of romance, they think of flowers, candlelight, moon-lit walks, soft music and exotic cities. But the most romantic moments in life are rarely scripted. Real romance is often spontaneous, sparked by a simple touch, a glance or even a smile. Romance is not a place that can be found on the map. You can't buy a ticket to arrive by plane, boat or train. Romance can only be reach by traveling down the pathways to the heart.

"Romance"

Someone told me it had died
That romance lived no more
The tears rolled down my grieving face
As I ran through their door

I looked for it on a garden path
With flowers fresh and sweet
And in a horse-drawn carriage
Strolling slowly down the street

I looked for it in a mountain lodge
Amidst snowy mounds of white
And on a beach at midnight
Painted with a full moon's light

It wasn't in a cable car
In the city by the bay
Nor was it at Niagara Falls
Where lovers like to play

I looked for in it Paris
In New York and then in Rome
I looked for it in Bermuda
Before I sadly headed home

I turned on the light and went inside
To find a sweet surprise
Romance was indeed alive
And living in your eyes

Sleep Tight, My Little Darling

One of my favorite poems, "Sleep Tight My Little Darling," evokes a familiar endearing feeling, as do many of our favorite lullabies. I would sometimes recite this poem to my son as he was falling asleep, wondering where his dreams would take him.

"Sleep Tight, My Little Darling"

Sleep tight, my little darling
May your dreams take off in flight
As you cuddle to your pillow
Your face glows softly by night-light

I kiss your forehead gently
As to not disturb your dreams
Maybe you could bring me back
A rainbow or some moonbeams

Sleep tight, my little darling
May your dreams be just as sweet
As the child here before me
Nestled gently in the sheets

Smiling From Above

"Smiling From Above" was written shortly before the passing of a grandmother, Grace. My father had asked if I could write something for her impending service since she was such a big fan of my poetry. My answer was yes, but my challenge was in writing something uplifting and inspirational. After all, that's what I write: uplifting and inspirational poetry; I don't do death. Well, after a lot of contemplation, I think I found a way to do both.

"Smiling From Above"

I stare into the twilight
And feel the shadows creeping near
But the darkness won't envelope me
For this I have no fear

His light will shine upon me
And for His guidance I will pray
As I join him in the Kingdom
Of that ever-lasting day

His arms will open wide
And encircle me with love
As I continue on my journey
Smiling from above

Something Did Survive

When a romance ends, most lose more than a lover; they also lose a friend -- usually a best friend. And in this time of such anguish, it's impossible to turn to your friend for comfort because they are the cause of your pain. In my own experiences, I found the loss of that friendship to be the worst part of a break-up. Having the ability to rebuild a friendship often seems impossible at first, but it can help heal some of the wounds.

"Something Did Survive"

With a fury loud as thunder
Our world was torn apart
Hurling chards of broken dreams flew out
From our shattered hearts
But you weren't just a lover
You were also my best friend
Until that fateful day arrived
When it all came to an end
I couldn't cry upon your shoulder
Or lay in your arms until dawn
For when I lost your love I knew
Our friendship, too, was gone
So many times I thought of you
And longed to hear your voice
To ask how things were going
But I felt I had no choice
No choice because our friendship perished
With the love we shared
That was until I saw your face
And learned we both still cared
You had felt the same way
And you, too, missed your best friend
As we talked and listened,
We felt our hearts begin to mend
Amidst the pain and heartbreak
We learned something did survive
Although it wasn't quite the same
Our friendship was alive

The Mistletoe

The concept of a traveling sprig of mistletoe sprang to life when I remembered a holiday party in college. In the corner of the room, among the decorations and gifts, was a small bench with mistletoe dangling down from the ceiling. I spent most of the evening plotting to lure a certain young man beneath it so I could make my move. But by the time I'd gotten up my nerve, the mistletoe was gone. It had been stolen and I was heartbroken. Fortunately, it turned out I didn't really need that silly little plant after all. As far as I know they never did find it, but I had fun imagining the stories it could have told.

"The Mistletoe"

Dangling from the ceiling by a little piece of string
Hung a sprig of mistletoe with all the promise it could bring
Although just only seven, young John knew what to do
He ran quickly from beneath it
When approached by his Aunt Sue

And when she wasn't looking
Young John tore that plant right down
Then smiled as he watched it drop quickly to the ground
Heather saw it lying there and picked it off the floor
Then beamed as she thought about the man whom she adored

For her it was the courage to give Mark their first real kiss
And reveal her deepest feelings in hopes
They'd share a new found bliss
She found Mark at the window watching kids play in the snow
And when she opened up her heart to him
His face began to glow

As they kissed, the mistletoe was passed to Cousin Dwight
Who had argued with his wife
But now believed that she was right
He asked for her forgiveness and raised up that mistletoe
She answered with a smile and a kiss both long and slow

The sprig was left upon a table
Then was snatched up by Aunt Sue
Who found young John
And gave to him the kiss so overdue

The Night

One night I awoke at three in the morning fully alert. After a few minutes of trying to go back to sleep, I couldn't help but enjoy my surroundings. It was dead quiet – no telephones ringing, people talking, televisions blaring, cars racing down the street. I stood out on my balcony basking in the cool night breeze and the dim glow of the streetlights. It was truly a peaceful experience – one that made me wish insomnia could always be so enjoyable.

"The Night"

Darkness drifts gently over the town
Slowly washing the daylight away
Streetlights illuminate a barren sidewalk
As it come to the close of the day

A story before bedtime
Or a cup of chamomile tea
Inviting weary souls to rest
Daytime sounds begin to fade
While a baby slumbers on daddy's chest

Lovers bathe in a full moon's glow
Stars twinkle brightly up above
As countless wishes are sent up
By those in search of love

Tomorrow's just a fantasy
'Til sunlight burns the night away
Birds chirp rejoicing
Another dawning of a day

The Night Breeze

In the deepest recesses of our minds, we have memories which never seem to diminish. Once again, we can feel a gentle caress, inhale the scent of their skin, and see the sparkle in their eyes even when it's not really there. It can take us back to a life we no longer know while providing us with the comfort and strength to make it through our present and future.

"The Night Breeze"

In the quiet stillness of the night
A breeze gently stirs the leaves on the trees
And your memory drifts into my mind
You are with me once again
I can almost smell your sweet scent lingering in the air
And feel your touch brushing softly against my skin
I close my eyes and see your beautiful face looking at mine
With a smile that treats my wounded heart with a healing salve
If only I could press your lips to mine one more time
And hear your voice that keeps playing in my mind
Like a favorite song I never want to end
Did I just hear you giggle or was it my imagination?
Oh, how I miss hearing your laugh
I know you'll have to leave soon, but please stay with me
Until my eyes grows weary and I can no longer fight sleep
Then I will look forward to another evening
When the night breeze will return you to me
And we can be together once more

Three-Dimensional Me

"Three-Dimensional Me" is a poem that was actually inspired by another poem I wrote. While "Infatuation" dealt with idealizing an image of someone, "Three Dimensional Me" recognizes and embraces the whole personality and the paradoxes that live in all of us. I was intrigued with my own personal contradictions. In some situations I felt shy and insecure; in other situations, I was outgoing and confident. Sometimes I was content to follow the crowd while other times – most times – I was ready to blaze a trail into unknown territory. As different as I can be at times, I know I will always to true to all dimensions of my personality.

"Three-Dimensional Me"

I'm a dreamer and a realist
Brave and bold and scared to death
A leader and a follower
Simple and complex

Ruled by my emotions
But also by my mind
With vision crystal clear
On the days I am not blind

A beggar and a chooser
Who is restless and content
A caring person who's indifferent
A devil that's been heaven sent

Hard as stone and soft as silk
Locked in chains and flying free
Perfect contradictions that make up
Three-dimensional me

To Achieve You Must Believe

Life often has a way of tearing down our hopes and dreams. Every day struggles to just provide the basic necessities of life leaves little energy to aspire above the mire. It can be easy to give up when the doors are being closed – or slammed – in your face. But I know the answer to every question never asked will always be no and that success is never achieved by quitting. I wrote this poem as a pep talk for all, including myself, not to give up in the face of adversity.

"To Achieve You Must Believe"

Deep within your eyes
Lies disappointment tinged with fear
That all you want will not come true
And you fight to hold back tears

Hope is quickly fading
As the door slams in your face
Snatching up your dreams
Leaving heartache in its place

Acknowledge what you're feeling
But don't let it take control
Evict it from your mind
Before it invades your heart and soul

Your dreams will not abandon you
So don't abandon them
'Cause if you let that happen
Your heart will never mend

Attitude is crucial
If you're ever to succeed
Don't give up and know your dreams
Will give you what you need

To achieve you must believe
You are destined not to fail
Hold on to your precious dreams
Until the day that you prevail

To See The Night Sky

This is the only poem with which I've ever shared a writer's credit. My son came to me one night after looking up at the night sky and told me he wanted to write a poem with me. It was to be entitled, "To See the Night Sky," and it was to be about a star sending us a message not to give up hope no matter what problems we were facing. I guess he really is my child. It took a while to formulate the rest of the concept, but the poem was born due to his inspiration.

"To See The Night Sky"
By Lynn C. Johnston and Samuel Johnston

To see the night sky
Breathless beauty from afar
Clouds gently part the heavens
To reveal a twinkling star

By night, the star shines brightly
Giving hope to all who pray
And hang their hopes upon it
Tomorrow will bring a better day

But by morning light, the star is gone
Hidden by the pale blue sky
And all the hope of last night's dream
Valiantly struggles not to die

At last, the daylight fades
And the star boldly reappears
It twinkles as if saying
I was always here

Constant in the heavens
Stars remind me to believe
That dreams obscured by daylight
Need faith and time to be achieved

Truly Blessed

I am a firm believer in learning as much as you can from other people's life experiences. By observing the way others handle the misfortunes, challenges and even the blessings that take place in their lives, we can learn how to better deal with these events in our own lives.

"Truly Blessed"

When I found more pain in others
Than I found within myself
I learned what it meant to feel compassion
And my pain began to fade

When I found more forgiveness in others
Than I found within myself
I learned what it meant to feel peace
And my heart began to mend

When I found more belief in others
Than I found within myself
I learned what it meant to have faith
And my fears began to die

And when I found more love in others
Than I found within myself
I learned what it meant to feel truly blessed
And my spirit began to soar

We'll Never Be Too Far Apart

As with "A Clear, Bright Star," a recurring theme in my poetry is that physical distance does not have to compromise a relationship committed to survival. As long as someone's in your heart, they are never too far away.

"We'll Never Be Too Far Apart"

The morning light shines in my eyes
I awake but you're not there
I clutch your pillow to my breast
Yet there's no anger or despair

Although I cannot see you
We'll never be too far apart
Because you're always with me
In my mind and in my heart

Sometimes the pain of missing you
Seems just too much to bear
Until I stop and realize
No force could destroy the bond we share

Not space or time or distance
Could ever separate our hearts
No matter where life takes us
We'll never be too far apart

Winter Days

As a child growing up in New York, I spent countless winter days playing in the snow. I remember the snowmen and snow angels, the sleds and the skates – and the hot chocolate and warm seat next to a crackling fire that always followed. I also remember all the nights I spent with my nose pressed against the window searching the sky for the first sign of snow, anticipating all of the fun to come. Today, even the thought of a frosted window pane can renew some wonderful memories.

"Winter Days"

A beam of light pierces through the window
And beckons me to come
As I draw back the curtains
I place my hands on the frozen panes
Slowly wiping away the frost

A smile emerges from my lips
Through the glass I spy delicate snowflakes
Swirling gently in the breeze
As if dancing to a song no human can hear
Each one looking for the perfect spot to rest

As the ground below is painted white
Memories of winter days long since past play back in my mind
Snowball fights and snow covered trees
Catching snowflakes on my tongue
Racing downhill on toboggans
And skating on the ice-covered pond

Snowmen with long wool scarves
And snow angels with broad wings
All coming to the end as dark encroaches
Calling us in for the night

Our snow-soaked mittens and frozen toes
Would quickly be defrosted
By the warmth of good friends
A cup of hot chocolate
And the vision of more winter days to come

You Are My Hero

"You Are My Hero" was written as an ode to real people battling their real world problems. Real heroes are not Teflon cartoon figures able to defeat evil with their magical powers and unwavering bravery; they are imperfect people who battle their own insecurities and fears as well as the situation facing them. This poem was written at a time when several people in my life were going though emotionally challenging times in their lives. They had to cope with experiences no one should have to go through, but they did. They were able to rise to the occasion and became even stronger from their experiences. Their stories filled me with admiration and the knowledge that you don't have to be perfect to be someone's hero.

"You Are My Hero"

You lead by your example
You find strength where there was none
You stand by all that you believe
And you stay when most would run
You march to your own drummer
And you're faithful to your heart
You've made the hard decisions
That would tear the rest of us apart
You could've crumbled from the pressure
When life broke your heart in two
Instead you fought with all your might
Until your skies returned to blue
A modest soul you'll always have
Without your accolades in tow
You claim you're nothing special
But you're wrong; you are my hero
You struggle like we all do
Through this experience called life
Yet your grace and your tenacity
Inspire me to rise above the strife
Like a Phoenix you have risen
From the ashes and the flames
You've stood up even when
You had to take the blame
Your life has not been easy
But somehow you've made it through
You'll always be my hero
And I'm awfully proud of you

You Make Me Smile

If you're a Dave Koz fan, you probably recognize the title. This poem was, in part, inspired by him and his incredible mother, Audrey. Both have been so kind to me and Audrey was particularly supportive of my poetry. She always took the time to pass along her encouraging words. Not everybody does that. I personally admire the people who know the most valuable assets in life will never appear on a financial statement.

"You Make Me Smile"

In a world that can get crazy
Where values often go astray
It's easy to forget what counts
As we struggle through each day

But sometimes on the road of life
You get to meet someone who cares
Who remembers what does matter most
The love and laughter that they share

They know nothing's more important
Than the love that's left behind
Making someone feel they're cherished
Building loving ties that bind

All their special loved ones
Reside deep within their heart
Yet they always share the pieces
So everyone can have a part

You are that special someone
Who only comes once in a while
And I feel blessed to know you
Because you make me smile

You've Become A Part Of Me

Some people have the ability of touching our lives in very special ways. Often they do so without ever realizing the affect on our lives. They can shape our character and personality, our dreams and goals and our inner most feelings about our place in this world, ultimately guiding us in discovering who we really are.

"You've Become A Part Of Me"

As I look up from your picture, I can't believe that we're apart
I miss the touch of your embrace but I still feel it in my heart
The time we've spend together left an imprint on my soul
I feel your presence deep inside
When our distance takes its toll

You've become a part of me in so much that I do
I can't imagine who I'd be if I had not met you
Your faith in me has sprouted wings
I've soared up towards my dreams
You've made me feel so special like I can do most anything

Your love for me has kept the ground below me smooth and soft
I'll fall gently on a featherbed when I can't keep myself aloft
Your support has meant so much to me
It's the rock on which I lean
When the world becomes a frightful place
You make me peaceful and serene

You've shared your words of wisdom and all that you hold dear
You've helped to light my darkened path
When the sun would not appear
It's the little things you've given me that I will always treasure
Recalling all our memories brings more joy than I can measure

Your smile and your laughter
Will sustain me to the end
For I will keep them in my heart
Until we meet again

About The Poet

Lynn C. Johnston

Lynn C. Johnston has been awarded five Editor's Choice and two President's Awards for Literary Excellence for her poetry. More than a dozen of her poems have been published in several anthologies, including *Forever Friends, Timeless Mysteries, Antiquities, The World Awaits, Turning Corners and Bridges*. Lynn's work has been featured online at Blue Turtle Crossing and Mirrors of Expression, reprinted in inspirational newsletters and used by therapists in grief counseling. Her poetry has also attracted poetry lovers at several California book festivals, including the Los Angeles Times Festival of Books.

Originally from New York, Lynn is a graduate of SUNY New Paltz. She moved to the Los Angeles area in 1988 where she currently lives with her teenage son. For more information, please visit her website at www.lynncjohnston.com or view her poetry videos at www.youtube.com/lynnthepoet.

www.ingramcontent.com/pod-product-compliance
Lightning Source LLC
Chambersburg PA
CBHW031258290426
44109CB00012B/645